Mealtime in Madagascar

by Jim Harrison

illustrated by Eldon Dotty

PEARSON

Glenview, Illinois • Boston, Massachusetts • Chandler, Arizona
Upper Saddle River, New Jersey

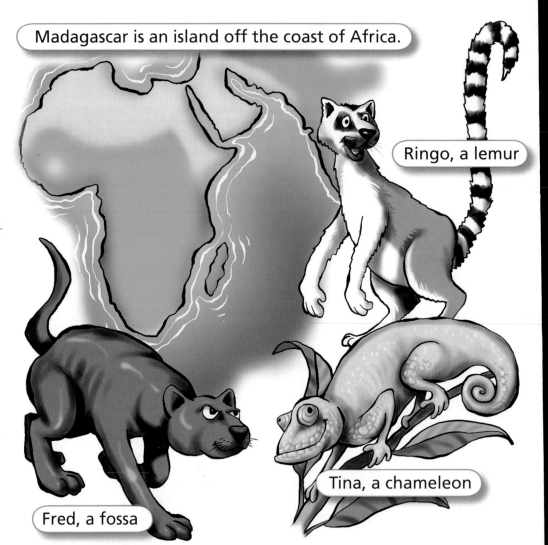

Madagascar is an island off the coast of Africa.

Ringo, a lemur

Tina, a chameleon

Fred, a fossa

Three animals lived in a forest on the island of Madagascar. Tina, a chameleon (ka MEEL ion), lived in a tree. She ate insects. Ringo, a lemur (LEE mer), ate leaves, fruit, and insects. Fred, a fossa, (FOSS a), was a fast, strong hunter. He ate other animals.

One day, Tina the chameleon was in her tree. Suddenly, she heard a loud noise.

"Who is there?" asked Tina.

"Ringo the lemur!" said a frightened voice.

Tina looked down. First she saw a long tail with black and white stripes. Then she saw a little black and white face.

"Where are my friends? Where is my family?" asked Ringo. "I don't like to be alone! I am scared!"

"Well, climb up here," said Tina. "We can look for your friends."

Ringo clutched a branch with his strong hands and climbed up the tree.

tongue

A moth flew by. "Time to eat!" said Tina. She stuck out her tongue—fast!—and caught the moth.

"What a long tongue you have!" said Ringo.

"Yes," said Tina, smiling. "I catch many insects with my tongue."

tail

Tina looked at Ringo. "You have a very long tail!" she said.

"Yes, I do!" said Ringo. "Tails are very important to lemurs. We hold our tails in the air. It is a good way to see each other."

Ringo ate a leaf. Tina was surprised.

"Do you eat leaves?" she asked. "Yuck!"

Ringo nodded his head. " Yes, and I eat insects, too."

Then Tina saw a tree branch move.

"Who is there?" asked Tina.

"Are you a lemur?" asked Ringo.

First they saw brown paws with long claws. Then they saw a brown face.

"Oh no!" screamed Ringo. "It's a fossa!"

Ringo scrambled down the tree and hid. Fossas really like to eat lemurs.

Tina the chameleon was angry. She becomes very big when she gets angry.

"Go away!" Tina shouted. "Get out of here!"

The fossa leaped over to Tina.

"My, you are a big chameleon!" said Fred the fossa. "Where is that lemur?"

"What lemur?" asked Tina. "There is no lemur here!"

"Well," said Fred. "I do not usually eat chameleons—but I am *very* hungry." He moved closer to Tina.

Suddenly, Fred could not see Tina any more! She had changed colors. Fred could not see the difference between Tina and the forest around her!

In the meantime, Ringo hid.

Fred looked down. "Where are you, little lemur?" he called.

Ringo was very quiet.

"Come here!" said Fred. "I will not hurt you!"

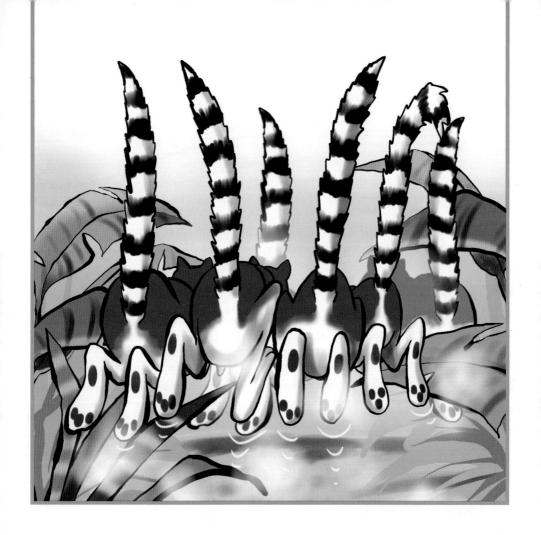

Ringo was very scared. Then he saw
five black and white tails. He ran over
to them.

"Ringo! Ringo! Where have you been?"
asked his friends.

"Quick! Run! There is a fossa here!"
cried Ringo. The lemurs all ran away.

Fred was unhappy. "There is nothing to eat here!" he said, and he left.

"Thank goodness!" said Tina.

A fly flew by. Tina stuck out her tongue and ate it.